VALENCIA

Text: David Navarro
Photographs: Digital Market and Photographic Archives of FISA-Escudo de Oro

Diagrams and reproduction conceived and carried
out in their entirety by the technical teams of
EDITORIAL FISA ESCUDO DE ORO, S.A.

Distribution: **DIGITAL MARKET**

VALENCIA

Valentia; that is what the Romans called this city. "Fortress" and "good omen", two meanings in a single Latin word. This was in the year 138 BC, though Greeks and Carthaginians had settled on the banks of the Tyris (now the River Turia) centuries before. Roman and, until the end of the 3rd century AD, Christian too. That was only the beginning, though, and Saint Vincent Martyι paid the ultimate price for this.

Then came the Barbarians and the Visigoths. In the year 709 AD, Islam entered peacefully until the Cid conquered the city in 1094, though the final assault was successfully led by King James I: This was in the year 1238, after a siege lasting five months. The Moorish population was replaced by Christian families, mostly from Catalonia and Aragon. This was the period when the recently-founded Kingdom of Valencia established its *fueros*, privileges and the *Llibre del Consolat del Mar*, the oldest written code of maritime law, was written.

In the 15th century, Valencia began to grow at a dizzying speed: a population of 4,000 at the beginning of the century had increased to 80,000 by 1483. This demographic expansion was matched by increasing trade prosperity, as, under Alphonse the Magnanimous, Valencia became one of the most flourishing capitals in Europe. Some of the most outstanding men and women

3

Valencia: aerial view of the old town.

Monument to King James I, in Plaza de Alfonso el Magnánimo.

of letters at this time were Jordi de San Jordi, Ausias March, Joan Rois de Corella, Joanot Martorell and Isabel de Villena.

The 16th century was marked by several calamities. The terrible floods of 1517, caused by the River Turia overflowing, and the plague in 1519, were only a foretaste of the disastrous was with the Germanies in 1520. Despite all this, though, the city became filled with Renaissance-style buildings. The 16th century ended with the expulsion of the *Moriscos*, Moors forcefully converted to Christianity, decreed by Phillip III. Given the importance of the Moorish craftsmen and farmers to the local culture, this was a crass error.

In 1700, Charles II died heirless, plunging Spain into a war of succession. Valencia declared itself on the side of Archduke Charles of Austria, but on 25 April 1707, the Bourbon victory at the Battle of Almansa ended the Archduke's hopes. Soon afterwards, Phillip V abolished the Valencian *fueros*.

During the War of Spanish Succession, known here as the War of Independence (1808-1813), Valencia put up fierce resistance against the French forces. In 1833, one of the Carlist wars ended with the abolition of the *señoríos*, the rights of the lords, and the closure of many convents. Moreover, two cholera outbreaks, in 1854 and 1855, each killed some 2,000 people.

Monument to El Cid, in Plaza de España.

Benicarló Palace, in Plaza de San Lorenzo. The palace, which dates back to the 15th century, has served as a grammar school, a silk factory and, during the Civil War, as the seat of the Republican government. It now houses the Valencian Parliament.

The importance of the population rise that occurred in around 1900 was due, above all, to the absorption of surrounding townships. The leading artists of the day included the painter Joaquín Sorolla, the sculptor Mariano Benlliure and the novelist Vicente Blasco Ibáñez. However, the city's growth was stunted by the general economic crisis. When the Civil War broke out, the legally-elected government moved to Valencia, where it remain from 6 November 1936 to October 1937. Franco's nationalist troops entered the city on 30 March 1939, and peace was declared on April 1, a peace accompanied by food shortages, ration cards and black marketeering.

On 14 October 1957, Valencia was hit by a devastating flood, after which the River Turia was rechannelled outside the city. The economy did not begin to revive until the 1960s, coinciding with a worldwide economic boom.

When democracy was restored, the Autonomous Community of Valencia was granted its Statute of Autonomy, which entered into force on 29 April 1982. Today, Valencia has a population of nearly 800,000 and is the capital of the Community of Valencia, as well as the seat of the autonomous government.

The Tourist Bus, or Bus Turistico, is an excellent way of exploring the city. Other possibilities are to hire a bicycle, to take a horse-drawn carriage or, simply, to travel by underground ("Metro").

WALLS AND TOWERS

The Quart Towers. The breaches opened in the walls here were made by French shells during the War of Spanish Succession.

Little remains today of the old Roman walls and the other, stronger fortifications built under Moorish rule. After the "War of the Pedros", Peter the Ceremonious built a walled enclosure whose perimeter tripled the extension of the Moorish city walls. Of the many towers and the twelve gates that once adorned these walls, those that can still be admired to day are the Serranos and Quart towers.

The gate in the **Serranos Towers** was built by the Master Pere Balaguer between 1392 and 1398. With an impressive exterior appearance, the interior of this building contains large openings designed to be used as galleries. In the 16th century, the gate was converted into a prison for nobles and knights, a purpose maintained until 1887.

The **Torres de Quart Gate** was built by Pere Bofill between 1441 and 1460. Its name is due to the fact that it lay on the road to the village of Quart de Poblet. This was a women's prison from 1626 until the 18th century. The towers themselves are cylindrical in shape externally, and flatter inside the walls. They are communicated by an arched doorway, formerly presided over by a custodian angel, and nowadays by the city coat of arms.

Keys in the lock of the Torres de Quart Gate. The building now houses a museum devoted to the locksmith's trade.

The historic, monumental Serranos Towers once guarded one of the most important entrances to the city.

The interior facade of the Serranos Towers contains large, arched openings designed for use as galleries.

THE MICALET BELLTOWER

Micalet, the famous belltower that adorns Valencia Cathedral, can be seen clearly from any point in the old town. Moreover, the 51-metre-high tower commands magnificent views over the city.

In 1381, Andrés Juliá began work on building a new Gothic tower that came to be known as the "Campanar Nou" or Micalet, after the popular name for the hour bell, which was baptised on the Feast of the Archangel Michael (the Catalan "Micalet" is the equivalent of "Micky" in English). The octagonal stone tower has four bodies or sections, the first three austerely decorated, giving the whole a rough appearance. The upper section differs from the rest due to its ornate decoration, with Gothic windows crowned by gables and rosettes. These adornments are completed by pinnacles crowning the buttresses, elegant tracery and refined sculptural work. The tower culminates in a terrace roof where the hour bell (Micalet) and the quarter bell are housed, hanging from a great stone belfry.

View of the Micalet Belltower from the opposite end of Plaza de la Reina. This emblematic Valencian tower is 51 metres high, the same distance as its base perimeter measures. An internal spiral staircase, with 207 steps, takes us up to the roof, from which the spire springs.

THE CATHEDRAL

Above all Gothic, but not exclusively in this architectural style, Valencia Cathedral is the faithful reflection of an important city, having undergone as many alterations as it has enjoyed decades of splendour. The cathedral has a nave and two aisles, all relatively low in height: the nave is twelve metres high, the aisles eight metres high. The crossing is covered by a dome, and there is a polygonal apse. It was built on the site of a mosque, itself formerly a Roman temple. Construction of the cathedral began in 1262, directed by Arnau Vidal. The oldest elements are the Palau or Almoina Doorway (1260-1270), whilst the Apostle Doorway, which began to be built in around the year 1300 is where the Water Tribunal meets at noon every Thursday except holidays.

The Chapel of the Holy Chalice (Capilla del Santo Cáliz), separate from the main body, was completed in 1369, covered by a starred vault. This is where the relic of the same name is worshipped. Only in the late-15th century was the corridor built that finally joined this exterior building to the Cathedral.

Aerial view of Plaza de la Virgen. An arch joins the Cathedral, seen here in the centre of the picture, to the Basilica of La Virgen de los Desamparados. Outstanding is the cathedral dome, a fine Gothic work, the first and second sections dating to the 14th and 15th centuries respectively.

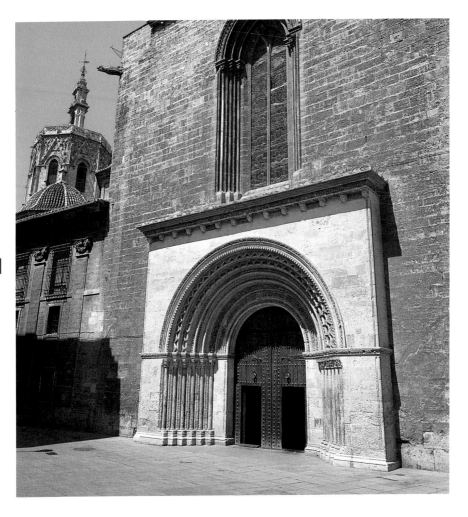

The Palau Doorway. The gable is supported by 14 head-shaped corbels that, according to legend, represent the seven marriages that took place between soldiers of Jaime I and damsels who came here from Lleida to repopulate the city.

The main front, known as Els Ferros (The Irons) due to the railing around it, was built in 1703. In 1744, the architect Antonio Gilabert Fornés directed alterations affecting construction and decorative elements with the purpose of giving the Cathedral a more uniform appearance.

The Cathedral Museum contains paintings by Almedina, Joanes, Goya, Jacomart, Alonso Cano and Orrente, as well as an interesting collection of relics. Amongst the marvels of the Catholic Church here are the arm of St Vincent Martyr and the mummified bodies of the Patriarch and other bishops.

The Holy Chalice. According to legend, this is the cup that Christ used at the Last Supper, later embellished with gold and precious stones.

Cathedral. The Tribunal de las Aguas, or Water Tribunal, meets before the Apostle Doorway every Thursday at noon. This venerable institution, founded in the late-11th century, resolves all disputes over the use of water in the fertile plains around the city.

Chapel of the Holy Chalice (Capilla del Santo Cáliz).

The Tower of Santa Catalina, seen from Calle de la Paz. Baroque in style, it was built in imitation of the Micalet Belltower.

OTHER CHURCHES IN VALENCIA

Though they cannot rival it for pure size and importance, some other religious buildings Valencia nevertheless approach the Cathedral in terms of age and beauty. These are the medieval monuments of Valencia, of which two are particularly outstanding: the **Church of Santa Catalina**, in Plaza de la Reina, and the **Convent of Santo Domingo**, in Plaza de Tetuán. Santa Catalina dates back to 1245, though it has been altered so many times since that we can find elements in all the most important architectural styles, right up to the present, in this building. The most interesting elements in the Convent of Santo Domingo, which was also built in the 13th century, and was converted to military purposes in the 19th, are the beautiful cloister, with finely-adorned Gothic arches, the chapterhouse and the Chapel of Los Reyes.

Other interesting churches in Valencia include the Church of Los Santos Juanes (Plaza del Mercado), the Basilica of la Virgen de los Desamparados (Plaza de la Virgen) and the Monastery of San Miguel de los Reyes (284, Avenida de la Constitución).

Nave in the High Cloister of the former Convent of Santo Domingo. Dating back to the 14th-15th century, the cloister has a ribbed vault, with a different design in the tracery on the five arches in nave and aisles.

Church of Los Santos Juanes: the front giving onto the market.
View of Virgen de los Desamparados, over the high altar in the basilica.

The **Church of Los Santos Juanes** was built in 1368. All that remains of the original Gothic structure, however, are the nave and the great blind oculus, as in 1592 the church was damaged to such extent by fire that almost complete reconstruction was necessary. The most interesting features include the Market Front, which is presided over by a sculpture of Our Lady of the Rosary. Over this is the clocktower, flanked by the two St Johns and crowned by the so-called "Sparrow of St John". The church interior is richly adorned in the imaginative baroque style.

The **Royal Basilica of Nuestra Señora de los Desamparados** is the church devoted to the city's patron saint, Our Lady of the Forsaken. Built in the late-17th century, the church features an oval dome supported by an irregular quadrilateral. Radiating off the central space are the various chapels and the shrine of Our Lady. The statue of Our Lady is a Gothic wooden carving that was placed on its side beside the deceased (the "forsaken") during funeral cortèges, which is why the head is inclined. The mantles and jewels that now adorn Our Lady were added later.

The former Hieronymite **Monastery of San Miguel de los Reyes** was built in the late-16th century. Once used as an asylum and then as a prison, the building was finally abandoned. Now, completely restored, it houses the Library of Valencia (Biblioteca Valenciana).

Plaza de la Virgen: Basilica of La Virgen de los Desamparados and the fountain representing the River Turia and its seven acequias (irrigation canals).
South cloister in the former Monastery of San Miguel de los Reyes.

GOTHIC VALENCIA

Before the city was taken over by the baroque style, long before Art Nouveau flourished here, there was – and still is – Gothic Valencia. The main exponents of this style are the Exchange, or Lonja de los Mercaderes and the Palace of the Generalitat. The Exchange, or **Lonja de los Mercaderes**, also known as the **Lonja de la Seda,** was built for the most part between 1482 and 1492 by Pere Compte. Its artistic and functional elements are in stark contrast with the strong walls to this building, which remind one of nothing more than a medieval castle. There are four parts: the Tower, the Consulate of the Sea, the garden known as the Orange Tree Courtyard and the Hall of Columns. This last, also known as the Sala de Contratación or market floor, is particularly attractive, with its helicoidal columns and magnificent vault, 17.4 metres high. Apart from its artistic value, the Exchange also shows the important position Valencia enjoyed in

Main front of the exchange, or Lonja de los Mercaderes, a jewel of European civil Gothic architecture that was declared World Heritage by UNESCO in 1996.

Lonja: spiral staircase.

The immense Hall of Columns in the Lonja was used, until recently,
as the trading floor.

The Palacio de la
Generalitat, seen from
Plaza de la Virgen.

Mediterranean trade during the 15th century. Not in vain did this building house not only the place of business, but also the Consulate of the Sea, which imparted maritime law, and the *Taula de Canvis* (Exchange Table), established in 1407 by the City Municipal Council and which enjoyed great prestige due to its solvency and volume of banking transactions.

The construction of the seat of the Valencian government, the **Palace of the Generalitat**, began in 1421. Work started with the central body, in late-Gothic style. The palace is organised into three floors and is flanked by two towers, one built in the 17th century, the other dating to 1952, though it is in perfect harmony with the whole, despite its modern construction. The interior features a courtyard with Valencia Gothic staircase on one side, late-Gothic arches, the Gold

Gothic courtyard in the
Palacio de la Generalitat.
(Photograph courtesy of
the Generalitat Valenciana).

The Court Chamber, or Salón de Cortes de la Generalitat: one of the paintings representing the three estates, or "braços" represented in the old Valencian Parliament.

The Gold Room in the Generalitat, built between 1517 and 1538, is adorned by fine gilt coffering – hence the name of the chamber, the work of the master Genis Llinares. (Photographs courtesy of the Generalitat Valenciana).

Room (thus known due to the splendid gilt ceiling) and the Salón de Cortes, which also boasts a magnificent ceiling, as well as a profusely decorated wooden gallery.

The **Royal Boatyards**, or **Reales Atarazanas**, in Plaza Juan Antonio Benlliure, which now houses the **Maritime Museum**, is a building with five parallel naves supported by brick diaphragm arches, over each of which rests a simple tiled gable roof. The building, which dates back to the late-14th century, originally housed the city's boatyards, arsenal and navigational stores. Its original site, a stone's throw from the coast on the very sand of the beach, is difficult to imagine today, with the port and the buildings that line the coast.

The **Almudín**, in the street of the same name, was built in 1307 and restored in 1517. Its function was to store and control sales of wheat. The building has a basilical ground plan, with three naves, the central nave higher than the others. Built from solid stone, the high walls are attractively decorated with popular paintings. The site is now occupied by a centre where temporary exhibitions are staged.

But Valencia boasts not only Gothic buildings, but also bridges in this style. **Trinity Bridge (Puente de Trinidad)**, the oldest in the city, dates back to the early-15th century, though it was partially rebuilt after the 1517 floods. Three other bridges, **Puente del Real**, **Puente del Mar** and **Puente de Serranos,** are later, dating to the early-16th century.

Statues of Saint Luis Bertrán and Saint Thomas of Villanueva were installed on Trinity Bridge in 1906.

Plaza del Ayuntamiento.
View of the Post and
Telegraph Building.
The Ateneo Mercantil.

PLAZA DEL AYUNTAMIENTO

In ancient times, when this site was occupied by the Convent and Garden of San Francisco, no on could have imagined it would one day become the centre of a busy city. This is a relatively new square, dating to the early-20th century, a more pragmatic than aesthetically pleasing plaza. Nonetheless, it is surrounded by interesting monumental buildings such as the **Post Office and Telegraph Building**, which dates back to 1915, and two 1940s sites: the **Ateneo Mercantil** and the **Rialto**. And, of course, the **Town Hall**, which was not always located here, nor did the building always serve its present purpose, as until 1854 it was the House of Education (Casa de Enseñanza). The mid-18th century building underwent whole-scale refurbishing between 1906 and the late-1930s, when the façade, with its classical line and profuse baroque decoration, was added. Inside, a sumptuous marble staircase gives access to new rooms built as part of extension work: the Mayor's Chamber, the glazed, lavishly decorated Salón de Fiestas and the chamber where plenary sessions take place, into which light streams from above.

Colourful flower stalls make Plaza del Ayuntamiento an attractive sight.

**Town Hall:
main façade and
marble staircase.**

Housed in the Town Hall, the **City History Museum** boasts many important works relating the history of Valencia: Father Tosca's Plan of Valencia (1704), codices such as *El Llibre dels Furs* and the *Llibre del Consolat del Mar*, the banner known as *El Pendó de la Conquesta*, the Royal Flag ("Senyera") of Valencia, the Moorish key to the city, King James I's sword and the Trophy of the Conquest.

Town Hall: the ballroom, or Salón de Fiestas, also known as the Glass Room.

City History Museum: the Royal Flag (Senyera Real) of Valencia.

ART NOUVEAU IN VALENCIA

The city boasts a good number of Art Nouveau buildings. Known here as *Modernista* style, examples include the Central and Colón markets and North Station, as well as others, perhaps less important or privately owned.

The **Central Market (Mercado Central)**, in Plaza del Mercado, was built between 1910 and 1928 by the architects Alejandro Soler March and Francisco Guardia Vial to replace an earlier building, dating to 1839, which had become too small for the purpose. The ground plan adapts well to the irregular-shaped site it occupies, covering an area of over 8,000 m², its roofing resolved by innovative domes and inclined surfaces. The most interesting elements include the covering framework, reminiscent of great industrial architecture using iron, and the perimeter walls, adorned with ceramic skirts at the base and metal "mallorquina" tiles at the top. Even now, this is not only important artistic heritage, this is also a bustling market where the people of Valencia come every day, except Sundays, to select the finest produce from a huge range of foodstuffs.

The main façade and hall of the Central Market, which houses 959 stalls.

The Colón Market.

The **Colón Market** in Calle del Conde de Salvatierra was built between 1914 and 1942. The building, which was designed by Francisco Mora Berenguer, is remarkable for its openness, enabling those inside to see outside and creating a pleasant feeling of freedom and.

North Station (**Estación del Norte**) was built in Calle Xàtiva between 1906 and 1917 as a result of the city's growth. Designed by the Valencian architect Demetrio Ribes, the station's interior roofing, formed by a great marquee supported by a metal structure with articulated supports, was considered at the time to be a superb technological achievement. Also outstanding are the door to the original entrance, decorated with two mosaic panels by José Mongrelle, and the exuberant decoration in the vestibule.

The Colón Market: view of the main front and glazed tiles decorated with Valencian themes.

North Station: front and lobby.
View of the mosaic panels in North Station by José Mongrell.

Standing beside the station, the **Bullring** is not a designed in the Modernist or Art Nouveau style, but boasts classical lines. Nonetheless, we can mention it here due to its proximity to North Station. In 1850, Sebastián Monleón took over the project to build this arena, which took its inspiration from the Roman amphitheatre in Nîmes. Its structure forms a 48-sided polygon, whilst the ring itself measures 52 metres in diameter. The 24 rows of seats in the "tendido" hold up to 16,000 spectators, making it one of the largest bullrings in Spain. Here, too, is a **Bullfighting Museum (Museo Taurino)** which is very popular with the fans, as it boasts objects relating to this spectacle from the 18th, 19th and 20th centuries.

Other interesting Modernist buildings in the city include the **Asylum of San Juan de Dios** (Calle Río Tajo), the **Palacio de la Exposición**, the **Ordeig House** (Plaza del Mercado) and the **Gómez Building** (Calle de la Paz), all four by Francisco Mora Berenguer, the architect who designed the Colón Market; the **Asilo de Lactancia** (Calle Amadeo de Saboya); the **Sánchez de León House**, also known as the Island of Cuba (Plaza de la Reina); the **Casa del Dragón** (corner of Calle Somí and Calle Jorge Juan) or "House of the Dragon", with its unusual decoration, in the style known as Fantastic Medievalism; the **Ortega House** (Gran Vía del Marqués del Turia); and the **Punt de Gantxo House** (Plaza de Almoina), with its peculiar white on red decoration.

View of the Palacio de la Exposición (Exhibition Palace).
View of the Ortega House, in Gran Via del Marqués del Turia.

SIGHTS IN THE OLD TOWN

Marvellous of urban development such as **Plaza de la Virgen** and **Plaza de la Reina**, with their monuments and pavement cafés, attract locals and visitors alike. The charm of the streets around these squares has also been further enhanced recently, as many of them have been made into pedestrian streets. If forced to choose just one, however, many would plump for **Calle dels Cavallers** ("Knights' Street"), which is flanked by great old houses, mostly in the Gothic style.

More charming nooks and crannies: Plaza Nueva, also known as Plaza del Cid, later known as **Plaza Redonda** or "Clot", was built by Salvador Escrig in 1840 on a site in the city that had since ancient times been linked to small business, and is now devoted, above all, to the sale of clothing. This is a circular indoor plaza with three blocks of housing in a uniform style. On Sundays, the square is transformed into a colourful market where the most unusual articles are sold.

At the end of Calle Colón is **Plaza Porta del Mar**, featuring a 1946 reproduction of the old Puerta del Real, or Royal Gate, in ancient times the last to close every night, leaving so

Plaza de la Virgen.

Aerial view of Plaza de la Reina.

Plaza Redonda.

A passage adjoining Plaza de la Reina.
There are many pavement cafés in the old town where visitors can enjoy a drink.

The "pouet" (little well)
of San Vicente Ferrer.
Courtyard in the Palace of
the Almirante de Aragón.

many to sleep out under the Valencia moon. The name of the square alludes to the old Sea Gate, or Puerta del Mar, which communicated the city with the local fishing villages and the port area.

The **Birthplace of St Vincent Ferrer**, a house in Callejón del Pouet de Sant Vicenç, boasts a tiny courtyard decorated with 18th-century *azulejos*, glazed tiles featuring scenes from the life of the saint, and a fountain once fed by a well whose water was supposed to work miracles, though it ceased to flow of its own account in 1975. Here, too, is the room where the saint was born and a Gothic church with an octagonal ground plan built in his honour in 1955.

There are many charming patios or courtyards all over the city. Particularly lovely is that in the **Palace of the Almirante de Aragón** (Calle Palau), Gothic in style, and which rivals the beauty of that in the Palace of the Generalitat; the patio in the **former Convent of El Temple** (Plaza del Temple), neoclassical, in the building that now houses the Civil Government; that in the **former University** (Calle de la Nau), neoclassical, adorned with the statue of the Valencian humanist Lluís Vives, who studied here; and that of **El Patriarca College** (Calle de la Nau), Renaissance in style, and also presided over by a statue, in this case that of the founder, St John of Ribera, by Mariano Benlliure in 1896. But other surprises also await in these last two buildings. The former university, founded in 1499 although completely reconstructed after the War of Independence, houses an extraordinary library whose collections include the first book printed in Spain, entitled *Les trobes in laors de la Verge Maria* (1474), and three first editions of *Tirant lo Blanch* (1490),

Courtyard in the former Convent of El Temple, built on the same site as the House of the Knights Templar, hence its name.

Courtyard of the College of El Patriarca, with 56 marble columns each carved from a single stone, brought from Genoa and decorated with a frieze of glazed tiles in relief (16th century).

the knightly romance written by Joanot Martorell and praised by Cervantes in *Don Quijote*. In the Patriarca College, where young men are prepared for priesthood, are many admirable works of art: the church, frescoes by Bartolomé Matarana, Francisco Ribalta's painting of The Last Supper and a polychrome statue of Our Lady, La Purísima, carved by Gregorio Hernández; and in the college museum, paintings by Joan de Joanes, El Greco, Francisco Ribalta and early Flemish artists, as well as many interesting documents, including original manuscripts by Lope de Vega and a rich collection of Bibles.

Church of El Patriarca: "The Last Supper", by Francisco Ribalta. Museum of El Patriarca: "Adoration of the Shepherds", by El Greco.

MUSEUMS

Opened to the public in 1989 with the mission of promoting research and understanding of 20th-century art, in the space of a few short years the **IVAM** (Instituto Valenciano de Arte Moderno) has become one of the leading contemporary art centres in Europe. The IVAM occupies two sites: the Julio González Centre, a new building in Calle Guillem de Castro, and the Carmen Centre, housed in a former Carmelite convent in Calle Museo. Apart from organising temporary exhibitions, the IVAM also has its own collections, one of the most important of which is devoted to the painter, sculptor and draughtsman Julio González.

MUVIM (Valencian Museum of the Enlightenment and Modernism), which opened in 2001, is also devoted to hosting innovative exhibitions, and these have attracted large numbers of visitors in recent years. The museum stands in Calle Guillem de Castro, housed in a building designed by the Seville architect Guillermo Vázquez Consuegra, itself one of the finest examples of contemporary architecture in the city.

The **Museum of Fine Arts** stands in Calle San Pío V, housed in a historic baroque building. The magnificent

**MUVIM (Valencian Museum of the Enlightenment and Modernism): main front and library
(© Photograph by Rafa de Luís).**

San Pio V Museum of Fine Art.

painting collection here includes works by such Valencian artists as Joan de Joanes, Francisco Ribalta, Espinosa, Vicente López, Sorolla and Pinazo. Here, too, are such internationally renowned works as the self-portrait by Velázquez and paintings by Van Dyck, Murillo, El Greco and Goya.

The **Museum of Prehistory and Cultures of Valencia** is housed in another interesting building, the **Casa de Beneficencia**, which itself replaced the former Convent of La Corona in 1841. The most interesting elements in this building are its eight courtyards with glazed tile friezes and the church, which dates back to 1883. The centre, in Calle de la Corona, near the IVAM, was established as a result of the recent merger between the city's museums of prehistory and ethnology.

The **José Benlliure House-Museum** is also found in the vicinity of the IVAM, at 23, Calle Blanquerías. Built in around 1885, the house was acquired soon after by the artist José Benlliure Gil, who himself planted a charming Mediterranean garden on the grounds, as well as building a separate pavilion to use as his studio. The house is one of the main attractions at the museum, as it is a fine example of upper middle class homes in the late-19th century. The garden also boasts interesting glazed tiles illustrated on religious and folklore themes from the 17th to the 20th

Museum of Fine Art: room devoted to early Valencian panels, and the "Saviour" panel by Joan de Joanes.

Benlliure House-Museum: the artist José Benlliure's studio and apartment. (Photographs courtesy of the Casa-Museo Benlliure).

century. No less important are the collections of works by José Benlliure and his son Peppino.

The **Falla Museum** is another unique centre, housing the collection of *ninots* spared from the flames since 1934. The museum, which also contains posters, photographs and objects related to the world of the *fallas*, stands in Plaza Montelivete, near to the Palace of the Arts.

The **City Museum**, in Plaza del Arzobispo, takes visitors on a journey through Valencia's history since pre-Roman times. The very building that houses the museum, the Palace of the Marqués de Campo, is an interesting 19th-century construction. The visit can be complemented by a walk to the nearby **ruins of the Almoina**, which include Roman, Visigoth and Moorish remains, and to the **Moorish Baths**, which date back to the 11th century.

Another highly recommended visit is to the **González Martí Ceramic Museum**, housed in one of Valencia's best-known palaces, the Palacio de los Marqueses de Dos Aguas, in Calle Poeta Querol. The building's fame can be easily understood just by contemplating its sumptuous façade. Inside are apartments conserved with their original 19th-century decoration and the ceramic museum itself, featuring interesting pieces from Manises, Paterna and Alcora.

The church in the former Casa de Beneficencia almshouse is now used as a meeting room by the Museum of Prehistory and Cultures of Valencia.

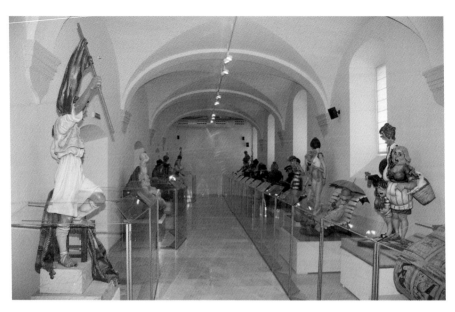

The Falla Museum (Museo Fallero) contains the "ninots" that are spared from the flames by popular acclaim each year. The Palace of the Marqués de Campo, which now houses the City Museum.

Front of the Palace of the Marquis of Dos Aguas, which houses the González Martí Ceramic Museum. The sumptuous façade was made in alabaster by Ignacio Vergara in the mid-18th century.

VALENCIA IN THE THIRD MILLENNIUM

Standing in the Turia Garden grounds, the **Palau de la Música** is one of Valencia's most emblematic modern buildings and one of the country's leading concert halls. José María de Paredes, the architect who designed the building, which opened in 1987, conceived it as a huge glass vault perfectly integrated into the gardens, landscaped by Ricardo Bofill. Here, then, are light, water and plants, in perfect harmony. Entering the huge lobby, we go through into the auditoriums themselves: a symphony hall seating 1,800 and a smaller space, suitable for chamber music performances.

The beauty of the Palau de la Música was not suited to housing the many congresses and conferences taking place more and more in Valencia, and it became necessary to build a **Congress Palace**. Norman Foster was commissioned to design a site that quickly became an emblem of the city after it opened in 1998. Outside the building resembles a ship's prow, formed as it is by a magnificent marquee supported by pillars of different sizes. From the air, the palace roof reminds one of a Watusi shield or a giant fish seen in profile. The facts and figures are equal-

65

Congress Palace.

The Exhibition Bridge, also known as the Calatrava Bridge, was built between 1991 and 1995.

ly impressive: 8,000 m² of zinc-coated aluminium floating over the building, extending 180 metros in a downward slope. The Congress Palace, in Avenida de les Corts Valencianes, has three auditoriums with total capacity for more than two thousand.

Two works by the Valencian architect Santiago Calatrava, **Exhibition Bridge** and **Alameda metro station**, form a singular work of engineering on the site of the old Exhibition walkway. The bridge, which is built entirely from highly resistant steel and rests on a single span, resembles nothing more than an extraordinary beam, slightly arched, crossing the river. The people of Valencia have aptly renamed this technical and aesthetic prodigy, which is 26 metres wide and nearly 131 long, as La Peineta, the ornamental comb.

However, the modern buildings that have contributed most to Valencia's international projection of later are those forming the **City of Arts and Science**. All share similar aesthetic qualities and the aspiration to create a great centre for scientific and cultural promotion. The site stands on the old course of the River Turia in an area measuring 350,000 m². Two internationally acclaimed architects took part in designing this extraordinary complex: Santiago Calatrava and Félix Candela. The former, himself from Valencia, is the architect behind most of the main buildings here.

The City of Arts and Science: Palace of the Arts Reina Sofía, and L'Hemisfèric.

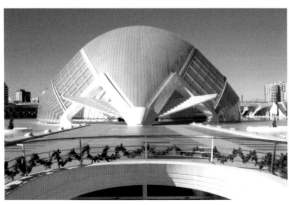

The Palace of the Arts Reina Sofía.

The **Palace of the Arts Reina Sofía** (2005) has four rooms devoted to art, music and drama performances.

L'Hemisfèric (1998) houses a Cine Imax Dome, a Planetarium and a Laserium, with shows projected onto a 900 m² giant screen. The building resembles a huge human eye which opens (and closes) to the world from the middle of its 24,000 m² pool.

The **Príncipe Felipe Science Museum** (2000) is a centre where visitors can learn about the latest science and technology advances whilst also having fun. A giant white concrete skeleton, reminiscent of dinosaur remains, "swallows visitors up", taking them down to enjoy the many attractions that await us amid its entrails.

L'Umbracle (2000) is a splendid promenade with a central tree-lined garden, affording the finest views over the entire complex.

The last works to be opened on the site were the **Serrería bridge**, in 2008, and the **Agora**, in 2009, both designed by Santiago Calatrava. The Agora is a huge, multi-purpose space, 70 metres high, with an area of nearly 5,000 m².

Finally, Félix Candela designed the unusual roofs on the main buildings housing **L'Oceanogràfic** (2002), a veritable underground city where visitors can discover the secrets of the planet's main marine ecosystems. The site, with ten different sections devoted to different themes. Here, incredibly, are 45,000 exemplars from 500 different species, in a space covering an area of 110,000 m², distributed on two levels. The upper level contains the central lake, play areas, sea mammal and turtle pools and an aviary, whilst the lower space houses 80% of the animal exhibits and the car park.

L'Hemisfèric.

The Príncipe Felipe Science Museum.
L'Umbracle.

L'Oceanogràfic.
Photographs:
Javier Yaya Tur (CACSA).

NATURAL VALENCIA, URBAN RECREATION

The **Monforte Gardens**, though favoured by the painter Rusiñol, are nonetheless little visited in comparison to other parks in Valencia. These neo-classical gardens, laid out in the 19th century, are adorned by bandstands, fountains and romantic sculptures, making this a delightful spot for visitors. The Monforte Gardens lie near Llano del Real, the starting point of **Paseo de la Alameda**. This gardened promenade, which runs parallel to the River Turia, is the most aristocratic in Valencia, its origins going back to the 16th century.

On the other side of Llano del Real, the **Real Gardens**, also known as the City Nurseries, comprise a large city park adorned with monuments and a lovely pond with ducks and other aquatic birds, ideal for strolling and for rest and relaxation. The gardens once contained the Royal Palace, which the people of Valencia themselves removed in 1811 due to the fear of French invasion. More recently, in December 2006, the zoo here was transferred to the Bioparc in La Cabecera Park.

Bioparc is a huge zoo designed according to the landscape immersion concept, that is to say, recreating the

View of Paseo de la Alameda and the Real Gardens (Jardines del Real).

animals' original habitats: the Savannah, Equatorial Africa and the Island of Madagascar. This approach enables visitors to see predators and prey in the same landscape, separated either by natural barriers such as waterfalls, streams and breaks in the terrain or by glass. The zoo houses some 4,000 animals from 250 different species, including gorillas, goats, lions, rhinos, elephants, giraffes, snakes, crocodiles, hyenas, leopards, anteaters, meerkats, mongooses, guenons, sitatungas, warthogs, rodents, tortoises and many birds and fish. Bioparc also takes part in programmes to conserve endangered species through breeding in captivity.

Standing beside the Palace of Justice, **La Glorieta Gardens** and **El Parterre** are another invitation to enjoy the peace and quiet. In La Glorieta stands the Fountain of Triton, in the purest Rococo style, whilst presiding over El Parterre is an equestrian statue of James I by Agapito Vallmitjana.

The **Botanical Garden** was installed near the old city walls in Calle Beato Gaspar Bono during the 18th century, when the ideas defended by the Enlightenment began to bear fruit. The gardens contain important botanical collections including some three thousand species of plants and trees from the five continents. Particularly outstanding are the tropical palms and other trees and the cacti and other desert plants.

La Glorieta Gardens: Fountain of Triton.
Botanical Garden.

**The Turia Gardens.
Typical barraca hut in La
Albufera.**

The Plan Sur ("South Plan") was drawn up in the response to the last floods to hit the city in 1957, reaping a terrible toll in death and destruction. Under the plan, the River Turia was rechannelled three kilometres to the south. This work, which was completed in 1973, left a space nearly ten kilometres long from the old river course, and it was here that the **Turia Gardens** were established.Little by little, from October 9 Bridge to Astilleros Bridge, not only parks and gardens and sports facilities have been established in this 15-hectare space, but also cultural centres such as the **Museum of the History of Valencia**, housed in an old water deposit, and the aforementioned City of Arts and Science, not forgetting **Gulliver Park** with its unusual slides.

Recently opened to the public is the **Polífilo Garden**, near the Congress Palace. This park was designed by the landscape gardener Carmen Añon, who took her inspiration from Francesco de Coloma's book Hypnerotomachia Poliphili: The Strife of Love in a Dream. Here, dreamlike landscapes compose one of the most relaxing parks in the city.

Finally, we must mention the **Albufera wetlands**, 15 kilometres from the city and one of the most important natural attractions in the entire Community of Valencia. Designated as a Natural Park in 1986, these wetlands cover an area of 21,000 hectares, including a 2,837- hectare lake. Here, visitors can take boat trips evoking the books of Blasco Ibáñez, glimpsing evocative *barraca* huts, the near-mythical dwellings of the men and women who turned the area around Valencia into one of the most fertile in Spain.

**Gulliver Park,
where children will
love recreating one
of the final scenes in
Jonathan Swift's great
novel.**

A CITY OPEN TO THE SEA

Just a few minutes from the city centre, well communicated, are **Las Arenas and La Malvarrosa beaches**. Both have been favourite places for Valencians to enjoy a day out since the 19th century. Nonetheless, only a lucky few could build houses here in order to avoid the tram ride to the beach. One such was the novelist Vicente Blasco Ibáñez, who built a chalet in Calle Isabel de Villena in 1902. This holiday villa has now been converted into the **Blasco Ibáñez House-Museum**.

The **Sea Front promenade (Paseo Marítimo)**, built in the 1990s, symbolises the union between Valencia and the sea. The two began to come together in the 18th century, when Avenida del Puerto was opened up. To the north, Paseo Marítimo links up with the town of **Alboraia**, with its interesting Port Saplaya complex, whilst to the south, past the port, it stretches as far as **Pinedo beach**, with its excellent typical restaurants, and **El Saler beach**, famed particularly its crystal-clear waters.

The union between Valencia and the sea was further cemented on 26 November 2003, when the city was designated in Geneva as the venue for the **America's Cup**

Chalet of the writer Vicente Blasco Ibáñez.

2007. This designation gave Valencia the honour of being the first European city to host the competition since it was first established over 150 years ago. Needless to say, the importance of this event requires works on a suitably grand scale, and a project was quickly launched to convert the port area into a "balcony over the sea", prolonging the sea front. The harbour basin was also improved as part of this development plan, and was restructured to enable the team bases to be installed around it in circular fashion. Around the bases, one of the most outstanding and emblematic works under the project is the construction of a dock for superyachts, which will stretch out 250 metres towards the centre of the harbour waters.

The other important works in the port include the dyke and the canal, which crosses the South (Levante) Dock and connects it with the interior marina. At the same time, the port was also converted into an attractive urban leisure area, with such new buildings as **Veles e Vents**, and the **AC Park** leisure park, a 107,000 m² complex including an amphitheatre. Beside, them several older buildings have also been conserved, such as the **Maritime Station**, built in 1914, with its characteristic clocktower, and the so-called **Tinglados** (warehouses), built in 1910 by Demetrio Ribes and adorned with Art Nouveau ceramic work.

The sea front, or Paseo Maritimo.

The Port of Valencia has undergone in-depth transformation in recent years to turn it into a place for leisure activities. Now, side-by-side with new walks and modern facilities are the

so-called "Tinglados", warehouses, with their Art Nouveau decoration, built in 1910, and the Maritime Station with its characteristic clocktower.

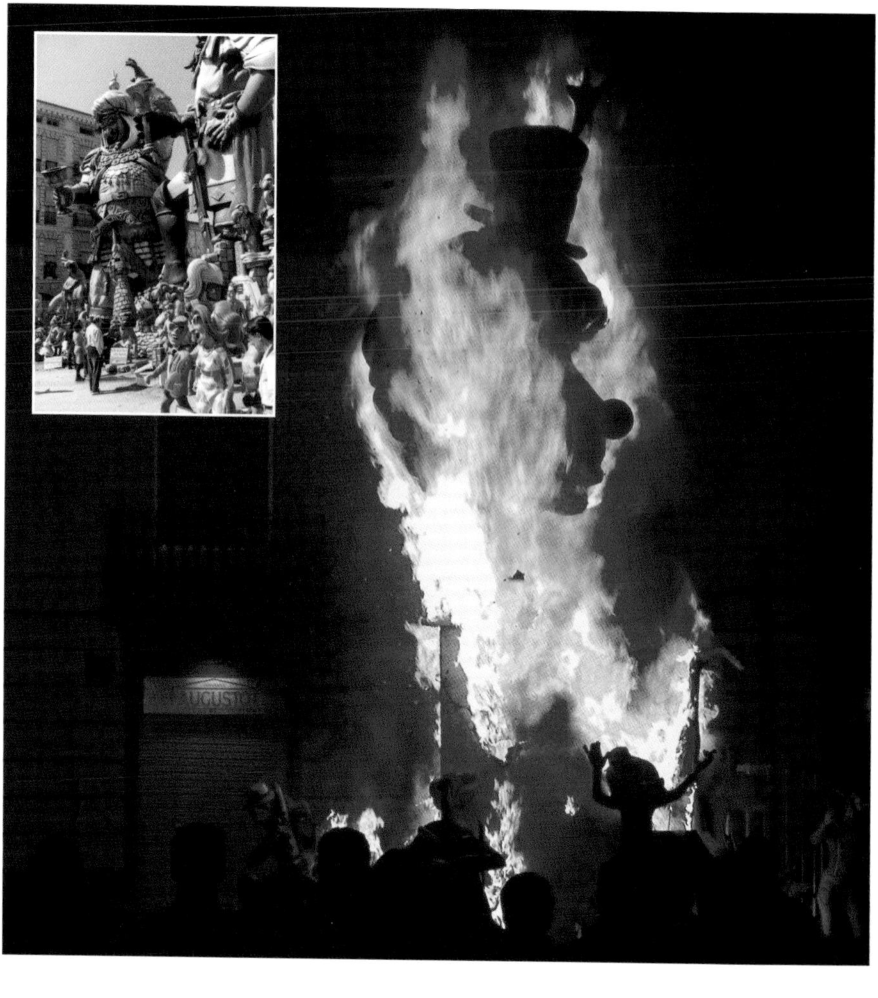

FESTIVITIES

One morning in mid-March every year, hundreds of fire-crackers go off all over the city on the River Turia to mark the beginning of the Fallas. This noisy awakening is known as the "despertà". The Fallas are the most popular festivities in the city and in the Community of Valencia and one of the most renowned in Spain. "Fallas" is also the name given to the monuments made from cardboard, plaster, wax, wood and other materials, festive works of art, that are installed in the main thoroughfares all over the city.

The Fallas take place between March 15 and 19 in honour of St Joseph. Every year, some 700 fallas are built in Valencia, some large, some smaller. They are installed during the "plantà", which takes place on the night of March 14, one week before which the local residents choose one *ninot* (doll) from each falla to be spared from the flames. The "cremà", which takes place on March 19, is when these splendid monuments are burnt to the ground. The falla outside the Town Hall is the last to burn.

Valencia's carpenters are said to have invented the Fallas. In winter, in order to work as the light faded, they used to light torches, which they would hang from artefacts known as "parots", a kind of candelabra with several arms made from logs or planks of wood. When the good weath-

Fallas: "Ninots" and the "cremà".

Around 700 fallas are assembled in Valencia every year. The motifs vary greatly, but they usually include recreations of "Moors and Christians" (one of the most popular festivities in the Community of Valencia), satirical representations of politicians of the day, and singers

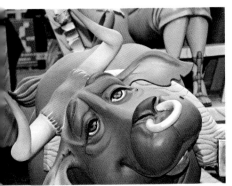

both fashionable or more classical, such as John Lennon. The first picture shows the children's "ninot" spared by popular vote in 2006, and as such inducted into the Falla Museum, or Museo Fallero.

Firecrackers ready for the "mascletá".

er returned, on the eve of St Joseph, they would burn these "parots" outside their houses.

Fireworks are an important part of the festivity, and displays take place every night in the old bed of the River Turia beside Paseo de la Alameda. The most important is the "Nit del foc", or night of fire, which takes place on March 18. Moreover, *mascletás* (firecracker barrages) take place in Plaza del Ayuntamiento every day until March 19 at 2 pm. During the festivity, there are also *mascletás* at some of the fallas at the same time.

Another interesting event during Fallas is the Offering to Our Lady, or Ofrenda a la Virgen. At this, the *falleros*, in their groups, or "casales", overcome their sleepiness and wait devotedly to pay homage to Our Lady of the Distressed, creating a huge mantle of flowers under here. The statue of Our Lady is carried out in procession on the second Sunday in May, when the people crowd around Plaza de la Virgen to carry Her on their shoulders and render all kinds of homage to Her.

Other important traditional festivities in Valencia include the Miracles of St Vincent ("Els Miracles de Sant Vicent"), the Corpus Christi procession of Las Rocas and the Night of St John.

One of the most popular and spectacular events during Fallas is the offering of flowers to Our Lady of the Forsaken on March 17 and 18. Besides traditional dances, there is also a magnificent procession of falleras in their elaborate, striking regional dress, carrying flowers to the patron saint.

FOOD AND DRINK

No guide to Valencia could fail to mention the excellent cuisine. Typically Mediterranean, these dishes are all based on the fruits of the earth and the sea. However, the chief ingredient is rice, which is prepared in an infinity of ways, though the best-known is in the form of paella. However, this dish can also be made in many different ways: with chicken and rabbit, with shellfish, with vegetables… The range of rice dishes includes *arroz al horno* (baked with morcilla sausage, pork chops and chickpeas); *arroz a banda* (cooked in fish stock which is then served separately; *arroz negro (*with squid in their ink) and many more.

Almost as famed as paella is *fideuá*, made with noodles instead of rice.

And for dessert, what better than delicious Valencia oranges? Like rice, oranges were introduced here by the Moors. Another sweetmeat not to be missed are *buñuelos* (fritters), particularly during the Feast of St Joseph.

Finally, no drink could be more refreshing than the local *horchata* (made from *chufas*, tigernuts; horchata from Alboraia is said to be the best in the world), preferably accompanied by *fartons*, another delicious local delicacy not dissimilar in taste to brioches.

Fritters (buñuelos) are especially popular at the Feast of St Joseph. Drinking horchata, accompanied by "fartons".

**Lladró
porcelain figure.**

ART AND CRAFTS

Valencia is legendary for its arts and crafts traditions. Ceramicists, glassmakers, carpenters and silversmiths, amongst others, have all left their mark on the city. Outstanding amongst the names that have continued their forefathers' traditions moreover, is that of Lladró, which produces world-famous porcelain figures. Many local arts and crafts products are on show at the Community of Valencia Craft Centre in Calle Hospital, from hand-painted fans, their ribs carved from ivory or exotic wood to articles fashioned in leather, silk and wood.

**Plaza Redonda: a woman making lace.
Central Market: shop specialising in leather wine bottles and paella pans.**

CONTENTS

EDITORIAL
FISA ESCUDO DE ORO, S.A.
www.eoro.com

I.S.B.N. 978-84-378-2639-4
Legal Dep. B. 1673-2009